A TASTE OF SERHEL

Family Recipes From Our Lebanese Village

Copyright Notice

Copyright © 2024 by Valerie Michael

Edited by Dave Hudson

Cover design by Day One Creative, Inc.

All rights reserved. No part of this publication may be reproduced, distributed, or transmitted in any form or by any means, including photocopying, recording, or other electronic or mechanical methods, without the prior written permission of the publisher, except in the case of brief quotations embodied in critical reviews and certain other noncommercial uses permitted by copyright law. Permission requests should be submitted to the publisher in writing at the address below:

HudsonMann Publishing LLC
PO Box 519
Belhaven, NC 27810
United States of America

ISBN: 979-8-9906395-3-9

A Taste of Serhel

Exploring the history and culture of our village, and the culinary treasures that define us.

Valerie Michael

Acknowledgements

To my cousins, Caryn Rishwain-Willett, Michelle Camping, Ann Pollock Smalley, Brenda Matte Butler, Denise Matte Zambeck, Jim Nehmetallah, Diane Nehmetallah, Helene Thomas Felgenauer, Michele Michael-Scott, and my brother Mark Michael, who so patiently answered my many questions, shared recipes from their families, and collaborated with me on this book.

To my cousins Kathy Witten, Terese Pollock, and Caryn Pollock, whose support and knowledge helped move this book forward.

And to all my siblings and many other cousins, a special thanks. You have inspired me throughout the years with your amazing grasp of our food, family history, and memories of our family that came from our village of Serhel.

Dedication

With great respect I dedicate this book to my grandmothers Manilia (Courey) Michael, and Kature (Jacobs) Michael, whose love for family, and our culture, were the inspiration for this book.

And to my Aunts - Margaret (Michael) Rishwain, Emily (Michael) Rishwain, Mamie (Michael) Pollock, and Nahia (Michael) Matte, who embraced the Lebanese way of cooking from their mothers, and who became the greatest Lebanese cooks I've known.

To my siblings because without you, I wouldn't be me.

And to my mother, Hazel Michael, who helped me with family history that may otherwise have been lost.

Introduction

In the heart of this book lies a rich tapestry of food woven with the threads of memory, courage, and resilience that characterized my grandparents' journeys from the serene mountain village of Serhel in Lebanon to the bustling landscapes of America.

This odyssey from the familiar to the unknown, driven by the pursuit of a better life, encapsulates not just a physical journey across an ocean, but also a profound emotional voyage. This is more than just a cookbook. It serves also as a bridge between past and present, inviting future generations to traverse the span of time and experience the essence of their heritage.

I hope each recipe provides a vivid picture of my grandparents' experiences, by offering a glimpse into the delicate balance they maintained — honoring their roots while embracing a new identity in a foreign land that became their home.

More than a cookbook, this is a tribute to the enduring spirit of those who dare to dream, a culinary homage to the rich flavors of Serhel, and a beacon for younger generations to keep the flame of their culture burning bright. It's a reminder that the stories of our ancestors are not just tales of the past but blueprints for our future, guiding us in preserving the traditions and values that define us.

Special Consideration

Lebanese cuisine reflects the pride of the country's culture, intricately intertwined with the different villages, cities, and regions of Lebanon, each presenting distinct flavors and nuances.

This book's focus is on the village of Serhel, exploring the culinary heritage of my ancestors, and the sincere manner in which they prepared meals for their loved ones.

While Lebanon is known to have many versions of any one dish, the recipes featured here are family recipes passed down from my grandmothers, mother, aunts, and cousins. It is my utmost privilege to share them just as they were shared with me.

About Serhel

Lebanon is located in the Levant region of western Asia in the transcontinental area of the Middle East. The country shares borders with Syria to the north, Israel to the south, and Cyprus to the west across the Mediterranean Sea.

Serhel, also referred to as Sereel, lies in the Zgharta District in Northern Lebanon, nestled in the Qozaya Valley high in the mountains at an altitude of 2,600 feet.

Throughout history, Lebanon has been conquered and governed by various powers, including Arabs, Crusaders, Mamluks, and Ottoman Turks. Before 1920, the country was part of the Ottoman Empire, enduring a lengthy occupation that began in the 16th century.

When my grandparents lived there, it was a small, mostly Maronite Catholic village with about 500 inhabitants. Even today, it remains predominantly Maronite Catholic. Villagers sustained themselves as farmers and shepherds, leading a simple, albeit poor, life in the tranquil mountains and away from the strife that besieged the country for many centuries. Still, Christians were considered inferior and treated poorly, some having to pay special taxes merely because they were Christians.

It is during this time of occupation that my grandparents decided to leave Lebanon and seek out their dreams of a better life in America. And the rest, as they say, is history.

"Yesterday is but today's memory and tomorrow is today's dream."

-Kahil Gibran

Contents

THE STUFFED STUFF
    Grape leaves... 16
    Stuffed cabbage rolls....................................... 17
    Stuffed mexican/grey squash......................... 18
    Lamb intestines.. 19
    Lamb stomach.. 20
    Stuffed eggplant... 21

STEWS AND SOUPS
    Green beans with lamb stew........................... 22
    Cannellini beans and meat stew..................... 23
    Lentils and noodle soup.................................. 24
    Chicken and rice soup..................................... 25
    Grey squash stew.. 26
    Eggplant and meat stew.................................. 27
    Green beans in tomato sauce......................... 28
    Chicken stew with potatoes............................ 29

RICE DISHES
    Lentils and rice.. 30
    Rice with mincemeat....................................... 31
    Chicken with rice and pine nuts..................... 32

BREADS
    Basic bread dough... 33
    Lebanese bread... 34
    Sugar bread... 35

Contents

STUFFED BREAD PIES
    Spinach pie.. 36
    Meat pie.. 37
    Flatbread with lamb..................................... 38

MEATS
    Kibbe raw... 39
    Kibbe baked... 40
    Kibbe in yogurt... 41
    Kibbe footballs... 42
    Skewered meat with spices......................... 43
    Skewered lamb with vegetables................. 44
    Boiled lamb tongue...................................... 45

SAUCES AND DIPS
    Eggplant with tahini..................................... 46
    Chickpea with tahini.................................... 47
    Garlic sauce dip... 48
    Yogurt sauce........ 49
    Tahini sauce.. 50

VEGETABLES AND DUMPLINGS
    Fried eggplant.. 51
    Spicy potatoes... 52
    Cabbage with cracked wheat...................... 53
    Chickpea patty..54
    Pickled turnips... 55
    Dumplings.. 56

Contents

FISH
White fish with tahini 57
Smelts 58

SALADS
Parsley and cracked wheat salad 59
Salad with fried pita bread 60
Tomato and onion salad 61
Dandelion salad 62

YOGURTS AND CHEESES
Plain yogurt 63
Pressed yogurt 64
Lebanese soft cheese 65
Cheese stuffed filo rolls 66

EGGS
Lamb with eggs 67
Egg and herb omelet 68

REFRESHMENTS
Rosewater drink 69
Lebanese lemonade 70

Contents

DESSERTS
    Sugar donuts.. 72
    Sugar cookies.. 73
    Filo pastry with sugared nuts........................ 74
    Date stuffed cookies..................................... 75

FAMILY FAVORITES
    Grandma's banana cake.............................. 77
    Grandma's lemon meringue pie................... 78
    Aunt Margaret's cheese pie......................... 80
    Aunt Margaret's chocolate cream pie.......... 81
    Aunt Nahia's potato cake............................. 82
    Aunt Hazel's applesauce cake..................... 83
    Pecan pie.. 84

The Inspiration for This Book

Growing up in a large Lebanese family was an amazing experience. With 26 grandchildren on my father's side, and 22 grandchildren on my mother's side, we were more like siblings than cousins and spent a lot of time together in our early years. Our home was always vibrant, filled with delicious food and lively conversations (mostly in Arabic with the adults) over dinner, coffee, and dessert.

Although immersed in this rich culture, we didn't explore our heritage much, overlooking details about our small village in the mountains.

Being Lebanese in the 1960s had its challenges, as Lebanon was not widely recognized. It was frustrating to explain my heritage when I, myself, was uncertain about who I was and what it meant to be Lebanese.

In time, I uncovered more about my family's past, discovering that both sides originated from the village of Serhel. They were farmers, shepherds, and blacksmiths, residing in modest homes without modern conveniences. Despite adversities and changing ruling powers, they remained steadfast in their Maronite Catholic beliefs. Reflecting on their lives in that era is truly humbling.

My paternal grandparents were married when my grandmother was only 14 and my grandfather was 17; they eloped, according to my father.

My maternal grandparents tied the knot when my grandparents were in their 20's. The story goes that theirs was an arranged marriage done to aid my grandfather's journey to America; a stipulation from his mother. Despite this, they stayed together for more than five decades until my grandfather's passing.

Arabic was frequently spoken by the elders in our household. Sadly, constant exposure did not help my siblings, my cousins nor myself, to learn the language, perhaps because it seemed so familiar that we never considered the idea of losing our comfortable environment. I presumed our ancestors, along with a plethora of delicious cuisine and the soothing sound of Arabic conversations, would always be part of our lives.

As my siblings, cousins, and I grow older, we are beginning to value the depth of our heritage. We are striving to unearth our roots by exploring our history, culture, cuisine, and some of us are even making an effort to learn the language.

This compilation of recipes originated from these ambitions. The determination to preserve our heritage and beloved cuisine has been the motivation behind this cookbook. I hope that this legacy will persist through our families for generations to come.

Valerie Michael

Spices and Herbs Used in Lebanese Food

There are many spices used by Lebanese Cooks. Regions play an important part in determining which spices are used. In our village of Serhel, spices were scarce due to the harsh winters, location of the village high in the mountains, and general availability.

Specific to the recipes in this book, we use
- Salt
- Pepper
- Cayenne
- Allspice
- Cumin
- Paprika
- Coriander
- Allepo Pepper
- Garlic
- Cinnamon
- Mint
- Bay leaf
- Rose water
- Orange blossom water
- Sumac
- Zaatar
- Molasses
- Parsley
- Basil

The Mezze

The Mezze is a prominent feature in many Lebanese households. Typically, a Mezze consists of a diverse array of small plates of food, enjoyed in a social setting filled with guests and constant chatter.

In my Grandparents' homes, Mezzes were a near-daily tradition, served at any mealtime or as an in-between. Common foods included in our Mezze were usually hummus, lebni, fresh vegetables, cheeses, olives, Lebanese bread, and coffee. For breakfast, eggs might be added, while lunch or dinner could feature fatayer and sfeeha.

Regardless of the specific dishes, every meal felt like a grand feast - an experience I always cherished.

Warak Eyneb
Stuffed Grape Leaves

Ingredients

Servings:		75 (approx. number of leaves in a jar)
Prep Time:		60 minutes
Cooking Time:		60 minutes
1	Jar	Grape leaves
2	Lbs	Ground lamb or beef
1 ½	Cups	Rice (washed)
½	Stick	Butter
½	Tsp	Cumin
½	Tsp	Black pepper
1	Tsp	Allspice
½	Cup	Lemon juice (you can use more for more tang)
1	Tsp	Salt
		Water (enough to cover leaves)

Directions

Mix all ingredients except grape leaves and lemon juice together. Lamb tends to be fatty so mixing may be a little difficult but it will mix. Add ice water as you mix so it is not dry. Do not cook.

Prepare grape leaves by washing. If using a jar, place leaves in boiling water for 30 seconds. This will soften any leaves that may be tough.

Cut stems off grape leaves. Begin rolling, placing approximately one tsp of meat mixture in the leaf with vine side facing you. Roll firmly folding in sides as you roll. Leaves should not be too loose or too tight.

Line the bottom of a deep pan with grape leaves. This will protect the leaves from burning in the cooking process. Use torn leaves if possible.

Place rolled leaves in the bottom starting with the outer edge of pan and place in circle. Continue circle until all leaves are rolled.

Add lamb bone for extra flavor. (I use a neck bone which I get from the butcher)

Pour lemon juice over rolled leaves. Place another layer of unrolled or torn leaves on top.

Fill pan with water to just above the top of the leaves.

Place dish over top of leaves to hold them in place.

Bring to a boil, reduce heat and cook for 45-60 minutes.

Leaves should be tender and rice cooked.

Mehseh Malfouf
Stuffed Cabbage Rolls

Ingredients

Servings: 6
Prep Time: 30 minutes
Cooking Time: 40 minutes

1	Large	Cabbage
1	Cup	Rice
1 1/2	Lbs	Coarse ground lamb or beef Lamb Bones (I use neck bone for flavor)
1/2	Cup	Pine nuts
1 1/2	Tsp	Salt
¼	Tsp	Pepper
		Cumin and allspice (to taste)
		Water (enough to cover leaves)
1	Can	Tomato sauce
1	Large	Tomato (chopped)

Directions

Cut core out of cabbage center. Carefully separate the leaves while running under warm water. With scissors cut large cabbage leaves in half, length wise, removing the thick center vein. Leave smaller leaves whole.

Bring 1 qt. water to a boil in medium size pan. Drop leaves a few at a time into water for about 30 secs. or until limp. Drain.

Wash rice, drain well, place in large bowl. Set aside.

Mix ground meat, salt, pepper, cumin, allspice and ½ cup water. Add rice and mix well.

Line the bottom of a 5 qt. Saucepan with stems of cabbage saved from cutting and lamb or beef bones.

Place meat mixture (about 1 Tsp) in center of cabbage leaf and roll tight. You made need to cut leaves if they are too large.

Layer in pan repeating several layers in a circle.

Pour tomato sauce over leaves and fill the rest with water to just above the leaves.

Chop a large, fresh tomato into small pieces and place on top of cabbage rolls. Weigh down rolls with a plate. Bring to a slow boil, reduce heat and simmer for 40 minutes or until rice and leaves are tender. (If you make a day ahead of time, do not cover with water or tomato sauce until ready to cook)

Koussa Mehseh
Stuffed Mexican/Grey Squash

Ingredients

Servings: 25
Prep Time: 1 hour
Cooking Time: 45-60 minutes

25	Medium	Grey squash
3	Lbs	Lamb or beef (Ground or finely chopped)
2 ½	Cups	Rice (washed)
1	Cup	Pine nuts
1 ½	Tbls	Allspice (may need to add more according to taste)
1 1/2	Tsp	Cumin (may need to add more according to taste)
½	Stick	Butter
1	Tsp	Salt
½	Tsp	Pepper
1	Can	Tomato Sauce or tomato puree

Directions

Clean squash by washing in clean tap water. Use vegetable brush if possible.

Core squash inside removing as much as possible and rinse again. Be sure to slice bottom stem off.

Saute pine nuts with a little butter, then mix all ingredients except rice and tomato sauce thoroughly. Make sure the meat mixes well with other ingredients. You may need to add a little water when mixing to keep meat from getting too dry.

Adjust spices according to personal tastes, then add rice, and mix thoroughly.

Stuff each one with meat mixture leaving about ½ inch at the top for rice to expand.

Place in pan with stuffed side up. Do not lay down squash in pan.

Add tomato sauce (fresh tomatoes or can of diced tomatoes can be use in place of tomato sauce) and water to fill nearly to the tops of squash.

Cover and cook on medium/low until cooked, about 45-60 minutes.

M'Sorrin
Stuffed Lamb's Intestines

Ingredients

Servings: 24
Prep Time: 45 minutes
Cook Time: 45 minutes

2	Whole	Lamb's intestines (you can buy these cleaned and prepped)
1 1/4	Cup	Rice, washed
2	Medium	Onions, chopped
1/2	Cup	Pine nuts
1 1/2	Lbs	Lamb meat, course ground
1	Tbls	Allspice
1	Tsp	Salt
1	Tsp	Ground cumin
2	Quarts	Cold water

Directions

Mix all stuffing ingredients together well. Refrigerate until intestines are cleaned and prepared. This will give it a chance for all seasonings to really settle in. Before using, taste to make sure no further seasoning is necessary.

Cut intestines into several pieces about 8-10 inches. Sew one end of each piece closed. Stuff the other end until piece is completely full. Sew this end until it is closed. I leave enough at each end to tie in a knot rather than sew. You can stuff by hand or use a sausage maker.

Fill pan with cold water, a little olive oil and salt in the water, and place on high heat. Bring to a boil and then lower heat for a slow boil for 45 minutes until rice is done.

NOTE: My grandmother used to sew both ends together forming a loop and then cut them apart after they were cooked. I use this traditional way in honor of her but as long as both ends are closed it's not a necessary step.

Ghammeh
Lamb's Stomach Stuffed w/Rice & Lamb

Ingredients

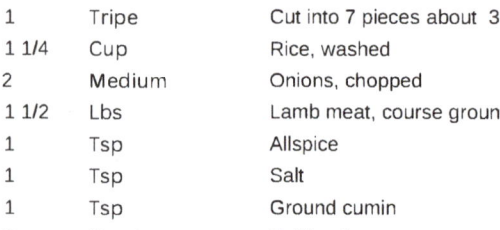

Servings: 7
Prep Time: 45 minutes
Cook Time: 1 1/2 hours

1	Tripe	Cut into 7 pieces about 3 x 4 inches
1 1/4	Cup	Rice, washed
2	Medium	Onions, chopped
1 1/2	Lbs	Lamb meat, course ground
1	Tsp	Allspice
1	Tsp	Salt
1	Tsp	Ground cumin
2	Quarts	Cold water

Directions

Mix all stuffing ingredients except rice together. Once mixed, add rice and adjust spices according to taste. Refrigerate until tripe is prepared. This will give it a chance for all seasonings to really settle in. Before using, taste to make sure no further seasoning is necessary.

Wash tripe and sew together on 3 sides leaving opening to stuff. Depending on where you buy your tripe, you may have to give it several washings before it is clean enough to use. I purchase mine from the butcher so it is relatively clean.

Once sides are sewn, put stuffing mixture inside. Fill well, then stitch up opening.

In a large pot put 2 quarts cold water and. a little oil.

Add stuffed tripe.

Raise heat to high. As soon as foam appears skim off well. Add 1 Tsp salt. Reduce heat to simmer.

Cook about 1 1/2 hours or until tender when pierced with fork.

Sheikh el Mahshi
Stuffed Eggplant

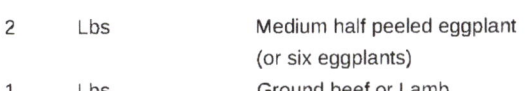

Ingredients

Servings:	6
Prep Time:	1 hour
Cook Time:	30 Minutes

2	Lbs	Medium half peeled eggplant (or six eggplants)
1	Lbs	Ground beef or Lamb
1	Small	Onion, finely chopped
2	Small	Tomatoes, peeled and diced or sliced
2	Tbls	Tomato paste dissolved in 2 cups of water
4-5	Small	Garlic cloves, crushed
1/4	Cup	Pine nuts
1	Cup	Olive oil for frying. (may use avocado oil as substitute)
1	Each	Green or red pepper (fresh)
1	Tsp	Allspice
1/2	Tsp	Cumin
1/2	Tsp	Cayenne (optional)
1	Tsp	Salt

Directions

Prepare eggplant by washing and peeling in sections so it is striped. In a deep-frying pan, heat oil and fry eggplant until it is light brown in color. You can also brush with oil and bake in oven.

Place on paper towel to drain.

In a separate pan, saute onion in oil until golden brown, then add meat and spices. Saute for 10-15 minutes until meat is well done.

Lightly toast pine nuts in a pan with a little butter then add to meat mixture.

On a baking tray, lay out prepared eggplant. Make a slit in the middle of the eggplant, then fill each one with meat filling. Do not over stuff.

Place sliced or diced tomatoes on top of eggplant.

Mix the dissolved tomato paste with garlic, add additional spices to taste, then pour over the eggplants until they are 3/4 submerged in sauce.

Bake in oven at 350 degrees for 30 minutes, or until eggplant is done. Do not let liquid completely evaporate.

Serve with rice.

Lubiah b'Lahem
Green Beans & Lamb

Ingredients

Servings:		8
Prep Time:		20 minutes
Cook Time:		50 minutes
2	Lbs	Lamb stew meat
1	Large	Onion (chopped)
1	Lbs	Green beans (French-cut work best)
1	Can	Stewed tomatoes (16 oz), or tomato sauce
1	Clove	Garlic
2	Cups	Water
1	Tbls	Allspice
1	Tbls	Salt (or to taste)
		Cayenne pepper to taste (Optional)

Directions

Sauté onion and garlic in small amount of olive oil until transparent. Add lamb meat and brown.

Add stewed tomatoes, tomato sauce, allspice and salt.

Cover with water and let simmer for about 30 minutes.

Add Green beans and cook another 30 minutes until bean are soft.

Serve with a side of rice or salad.

OPTIONAL: You can add red pepper to taste, if you like it spicy.

NOTE: I use frozen, French cut beans. They are already stemmed and more tender than regular green beans.

Fasolia bi Lahem

Bean and Meat Stew

Ingredients

Servings:		6
Prep time:		20 minutes
Cook time:		40 minutes
1	Lbs	Cubed lamb pieces and/or lamb shank or cubed chuck beef
1	Can	Tomato sauce or diced tomatoes
2	Cans	Cannelini Beans (Do not drain)
1	Tsp	Salt
1/2	Tsp	Pepper
1/2	Tsp	Cumin
1	Tsp	Allspice

Directions

Cover meat with water and boil until tender on medium heat (about 20 mins).

Add cannelini beans with liquid.

Add tomato sauce and all the spices. Add water if necessary.

Cover and cook at medium/low heat for about 20 mins.

Serve over white rice if desired.

Rishta

Lentils and Noodle Soup

Ingredients

Servings:	4
Prep time:	20 minutes
Cook time:	50 minutes

1	Medium	Onion
8	Cups	Water
1	Cup	Brown lentils
2	Cups	Flour
2	Cups	Warm water
1/2	Tsp	Salt

Directions

Rinse lentils, add to soup pot with onion, salt and water and cook on medium high until lentils are tender, about 20 minutes.

To prepare noodles, mix flour with warm water and 1/2 Tsp salt.

Roll thin and cut into strips about 1/2 inch wide and about 1/12 inches long.

Drop noodles into boiling pot with lentils and cook for 30 more minutes. Add more water to keep soup consistency.

Serve with Lebanese salad, bread, or Lebni.

Sharba djej ou riz
Chicken and Rice Soup

Ingredients

Servings: 6-8
Prep time: 20 minutes
Cook time: 50 minutes

1	Whole	Chicken
2	Cups	Celery, chopped
1/2	Cup	Rice
2	Quarts	Water
2		Bay leaf
		Salt and pepper to taste

Directions

Cook chicken until tender but not cooked through (about 10 minutes). Remove from water but do not discard.

Let chicken cool and shred for soup.

Return shredded chicken to water and add celery, bay leaf, salt, pepper. Let simmer for 20 minutes, then add rice.

Cook until rice is done, approximately 20 minutes

Mudfunet Koussa
Grey Squash Stew

Ingredients

Servings:			4 servings
PrepTime:		20 minutes
Cook Time:		30 minutes

1	Large	Onion (chopped)
12	Medium	Squash (Mexican or Grey)
1	Large	Canned Skinned Tomatoes
1	Tsp	Salt
2	Tbls	Allspice
1	Tsp	Cumin
1/2	Tbls	Black pepper
1	Quart	Water (more if needed)

Directions

Wash squash thoroughly.

Chop squash into chunks. Set aside.

Saute onion with a little salt and butter. Add squash.

Cook for five minutes.

Add tomatoes and spices, cover with enough water to get a stew consistency.

Cook for 30 minutes or until squash and tomatoes are tender.

Bite n'jan bi lahem
Eggplant and Meat Stew

Ingredients

Servings: 6 servings
PrepTime: 20 minutes
Cook Time: 30 minutes

2	Lbs	Cubed Meat (lamb or beef)
3	Medium	Eggplants (peeled)
1	Large	Onion (sliced)
2.	Tbls	Butter
1	Tsp	Salt
1/2	Tsp	Pepper
1	Tbls	Allspice (more if you like it spicy)
1/2	Tsp	Cumin
1	Can	Tomato paste (small)
1	Can	Tomato sauce (16 oz)

Directions

Season meat with salt, pepper, allspice and cumin.

Brown meat with onion in butter and simmer until meat is partially done. Add tomato paste and cook a little more on medium low heat.

Cut eggplant into chunks and add to meat mixture.

Cook continually stirring until eggplant is tender.

Add tomato sauce and continue cooking until meat and eggplant are fully incorporated.

Serve with rice.

Loubia b'zeit

Green Beans in Tomato Sauce

Ingredients

Servings: 8
Prep time: 20 minutes
Cook time: 50 minutes

1	Large	Onion or two medium onions
1	Lb	Green beans (washed and chopped)
1	Tsp	Allspice
½	Tsp	Cumin
1	Tsp	Salt
1	Can	Tomato sauce
2	Cups	Water

Directions

Sauté onions until caramelized. Do not burn onions.

Add green beans, spices, salt, tomato sauce or stewed tomatoes, and water.

Let cook until beans are tender, about 50 minutes.

Add more spices as needed.

Serve with Lebanese rice and salad.

Djej Yakhnee
Chicken Stew with Potatoes

Ingredients

Servings: 8
Prep time: 30 minutes
Cook time: 30 minutes

1	Medium	Chicken Fryer (cut into pieces)
2	Large	Onions (quartered)
1/2	Dozen	Carrots (cut into 1 inch rounds)
8	Large	Potatoes (peeled and cut into chunks)
16	Oz	Tomato sauce (can)
1	Tsp	Allspice
1/2	Tsp	Cumin
1	Tsp	Salt
1/2	Tsp	Pepper to taste
2	Tbls	Olive oil

Directions

Brown chicken on all sides in olive oil.

Place chicken in pot. Add onions, carrots, potatoes, seasoning and tomato sauce.

Cook for 30 minutes or until vegetables are tender.

Serve hot with Lebanese bread and salad.

Mujadara

Lentils and Rice

Ingredients

Servings: 6
Prep Time: 10 minutes
Cooking Time: 40 minutes

1	Medium	Onion (chopped)
2	Cups	Lentils
1 ½	Cups	Rice (washed)
1	Tbls	Olive oil
1	Tbls	Garlic (optional)
1	Tsp	Salt
4	Cups	Water

Directions

Add oil, garlic, and onions and saute until onions are dark brown (a little burn around the edges adds extra flavor).

Once onions are brown, add lentils and salt, and fill pan half way with water (about 2 cups). Bring to a boil on high heat.

Once it starts to boil, reduce to low heat, cover, and let cook for 20 minutes.

Add rice and let cook for 20 minutes or until rice is cooked. You may need to add extra water.

If there is too much water once the lentils and rice are cooked, turn off heat, uncover and let sit for a few minutes.

OPTIONAL: Serve with Leban, Lebanese bread, sliced onion, and red pepper.

Hashawi
Lebanese Rice w/Mince Meat

Ingredients

Servings: 6
Prep Time: 30 minutes
Cook Time: 40 minutes

1	Lb	Lamb (minced)
3/4	Cup	Rice (washed)
1/4	Cup	Pine nuts
2	Tbls	Olive Oil
1	Tbls	Allspice
1	Tsp	Sea salt
1/2	Tsp	Black pepper

Directions

Brown pine nuts in butter and set to the side. Watch carefully as they burn quickly.
Add olive oil in same pan and saute minced lamb.
Add allspice, salt, and pepper.
Add pine nuts when lamb is cooked. Mix thoroughly and set aside.
In separate pan cook rice. I use Uncle Ben's Original Rice. Do not use Minute Rice.
When rice is cooked (about 20 minutes) mix with minced lamb.

OPTIONAL: Add peas

Serve as main dish with Lebanese salad and bread or as a side dish.

Djej bi riz ou snoubor

Chicken w/Rice & Pine Nuts

Ingredients

Servings: 4-6
Prep time: 30 minutes
Cooking time: 1 hour

3	Lbs	Chicken meat (white and dark)
1 ½	Cups	Rice (washed)
¾	Cup	Chicken (thinly cut or shredded)
1	Cup	Pine nuts
3	Cups	Chicken broth
1	Tbls	Allspice
1	Tsp	Salt
1/2	Tsp	Cumin
1/2	Cup	Butter
2	Tbls	Olive oil

Directions

Boil chicken until done all the way through (About 30 minutes). You can season the water with salt, cumin, and allspice for extra flavor.

Cut or shred chicken. Saute in olive oil until slightly browned.

Add butter, pine nuts and rice and saute until browned.

Add chicken broth to cover. (approx. 3 cups)

Add allspice and salt. Bring to a boil then simmer for 20 minutes or until rice is cooked.

Serve with Lebanese Bread and salad

Aajeen
Basic Dough

Ingredients

Servings: 40 loaves of bread or
 40 Fatayer or
 60 Meat Pies
Prep time: 30 minutes
Cook time: 1-2 hours (to allow dough to rise)

4	Cups	All purpose flour
1 ½	Tsp	Salt
1	Tbsp	Sugar
2	Tbsp	Yeast (2 packets)
½	Cup	Vegetable Oil (They say don't use olive oil but I do.)
1	Cup	Warm water (add more as you knead)

Directions

Mix yeast in ½ cup warm water. This is part of your 1 cup total. Add sugar. Let it dissolve and proof thoroughly before adding to flour mixture. If mixture doesn't form bubbles yeast could be dormant.

Mix all dry ingredients, then add oil, yeast mixture and remainder of water.

Knead the dough, place it in a lightly greased bowl. Cover it and place in warm place. Let rise for one hour.

When ready, cut dough into desired pieces and form each piece into a ball. Cover them and let rest for 10 minutes. Then proceed with your stuffing. (Recipes separate)

NOTE: This is a basic dough recipe used for most dishes requiring dough. This should make 40 fatayer or 60 meat pies

Khubez

Lebanese Bread

Ingredients

Servings:		40
Prep Time:		2 hours
Cook Time:		5 minutes per loaf

Basic Dough Recipe, Page 33

4	Cups	All purpose flour
1 ½	Tsp	Salt
1	Tbsp	Sugar
2	Tbsp	Instant yeast (2 packets)
½	Cup	Vegetable Oil (They say don't use olive oil but I do.)
1	Cup	Warm water (you may need to add more as you knead)

Directions

Individual loaves can be frozen prior to baking. If you freeze, place sheets of parchment between each loaf. Thaw to room temperature before baking. You may need to flour again to keep from sticking.

Mannoush
Sugar Bread

Ingredients

Servings: 18-20
Prep Time: 1-2 hours
Cook Time: 5 minutes per loaf
Basic Dough Recipe, Page 33

Mannoush is thicker than the bread so this will make about 18-20 Mannoush

4	Cups	All-purpose flour
1 ½	Tsp	Salt
1	Tbsp	Sugar
1	Tbsp	Instant yeast (1 packet)
½	Cup	Vegetable Oil (I prefer olive oil)
1	Cup	Warm water (you may need to add more as you knead)

Directions

Mix yeast in ½ cup warm water. This is part of your 1 cup total. Let it dissolve and proof thoroughly before adding to flour mixture.

Mix all dry ingredients, then add oil, yeast and remainder of water.

Knead the dough, place it in a lightly greased bowl. Cover it and place in warm place. Let rise for one hour.

When ready, cut dough into desired pieces and form each piece into a ball. Cover them and let rest for 10 minutes. Then proceed with rolling. Each loaf should be about 1/2" thick circle.

Once it is rolled, poke fingers on top layer to make little crevices.

Pour some oil and add sugar.

Bake until dough is cooked through and slightly brown.*

NOTE: You can add cheese or zaatar spice rather than sugar for a more savory taste.

Fatayer Spanigh
Spinach Pie

Ingredients

Servings: 40 pieces
Prep time: 2 hours
Cook time: 10-14 minutes

Basic Dough Recipe, Page 33

Spinach Filling:

5	Lbs	Spinach (or 11 bunches)
11	Bunches	Green Onions
1 ½	Bunches	Parsley
½	Cup	Olive oil
¼	Cup	Allspice
4	Tbsp	Cumin
		Salt to taste
		Cayenne (optional)

Directions

Preheat oven to 450 degrees
Prepare Basic Dough recipe

Mix all ingredients for spinach filling together except olive oil. Phase in allspice depending on how spicy you want it. Once it is thoroughly mixed, add olive oil and mix again.

Once dough is ready, use rolling pin to form into a 5-inch circle.

Place spinach filling in the middle. Fold into a triangle and pinch closed tightly.

You can seal the edges with a little water. This will keep it from opening when baking.

 Place on oiled baking sheet, in preheated oven, for 10 to 14 minutes until golden brown. You may place under broiler for a minute or so to brown the tops but watch closely as they will burn quickly.

If you like a little heat, you can add red pepper to spinach mixture.

NOTE: Let the spinach mixture sit for a while and then drain as much liquid as possible. This will help prevent your pies from opening when baking.

Sfeeha
Meat Pie

Ingredients

Servings: 60
Prep time: 2 hours
Cook time: 15 minutes

Basic Dough Recipe, Page 33

Meat Filling:

3	Lbs	Ground lamb or beef (I prefer lamb)
2	Medium	Onions
½	Cup	Pine nuts
1	Tbls	Butter
2	Tbls	Allspice
1/2	Tbls	Cumin
1/2	Tbls	Pepper
		Salt to taste

Directions

Prepare Basic Dough

Saute pine nuts in butter until lightly brown. Set aside.

Cook onions until transluscent.

Combine meat and spices. Mix thoroughly and partially cook. Add onions and pine nuts and mix again. Cook until meat is done.

Roll out dough into 3 inch rounds.

Use tablespoon to place mixture onto prepared dough rounds. Fold in half to make half moon shape. Pinch ends closed tightly.

Arrange on oiled baking sheet and bake at 350 degrees F for 15 minutes until bottoms are light brown, then broil tops until lightly browned.

Lahem bi ajeen

Lebanese Flatbread with Lamb

Ingredients

Servings.		15
Prep Time:		30
Cook Time:		6 minutes

1	Lb	Lamb (ground)
2	Medium	Tomatoes finely chopped
1	Small	Green pepper
1	Medium	Onion finely chopped
2	Cloves	Garlic (optional)
1/2	Bunch	Parsley (finely chopped)
2	Tbls	Fresh mint (finely chopped)
1/2	Tsp	Cumin
1/2	Tsp	Cayenne
1	Can	Tomato paste (6 oz)
1	Tsp	Salt
1/2	Tsp	Black Pepper
		Flour tortillas or homemade Lebanese bread

Directions

Heat the oven to 425 degrees F.

Pulse the garlic in a food processor to mince it. Add the onion and pulse to chop, then add the green pepper and pulse to chop.

Add the lamb, tomato paste, tomatoes, parsley, mint, cumin, cayenne, and salt and pepper. Process until everything is very well chopped. The consistency should be wet and pasty, like hummus.

Spread a thin layer of the meat mixture onto flour tortillas (or homemade flatbread) all the way to the edge.

Bake directly on the oven rack for approximately 6 minutes, or until the edges are browned and the meat is cooked through.

If the tortilla begins to inflate in the oven, pop it with a fork from the top.

To serve, squeeze some lemon over the top, fold the pizza into quarters, and eat out of hand.

Kibbe Nayeh
Raw Meat w/Bulgur and Spices

Ingredients

Servings:		8
Prep time:		30 minutes (total)
Cook time:		Served raw
3	Lbs	Lamb or beef (I prefer beef)
3	Cups	Bulgur wheat (#1 or fine is best)
		Tublah
3	Tsp	Allspice
1	Tsp	Cumin
		Salt (to taste)
TUBLAH		
1	Medium	Onion
3	Medium	Red bell peppers

Grind onion and red bell pepper together. I prefer to grind tublah fresh for this recipe, however, you can make tublah ahead of time and freeze up to six months. The rule of thumb is to use 1/4 onion and one bell pepper for every pound of meat, however, you can adjust to your taste.

Directions

Wash bulgur two to three times and let it soak in a little water. I do this a couple of hours before I'm going to mix so that it softens.

Meat should be fresh (organic if possible), free of hormones, antibiotics or any chemicals. I prefer London broil as it has a good flavor but top sirloin is good too. Clean meat to remove as much fat as you can. Freeze meat for a day or until semi frozen.

Grind meat (semi frozen) two times in meat grinder. I grind my own meat so that I know the grinder is clean and not used for other meats.

Mix spices, salt, some bell pepper mixture into meat and refrigerate. I do this a couple of hours before serving so that the spices have time to absorb.

When ready to mix, put bulgur, one cup at a time and mix. Add more of the bell pepper mix if needed. Add more spices if needed. Knead all ingredients until they are thoroughly mixed. Add a little ice water as you mix to keep it from getting dry.

Serve immediately or refrigerate. May be served as a side dish or main dish. Serve with Lebanese bread and fresh onion, oilive oil and cayenne pepper.

Kibbe Syniah

Fried or Baked Kibbe

Ingredients

Servings:		8 or more
Prep time:		15 minutes
Cook time:		40 minutes

1	Lb	Lamb or beef (I prefer beef)
1 1/2	Cups	Bulgur wheat (#1 or fine)
1	Medium	Red Bell pepper
½	Medium	Onion
3	Tsp	Allspice
1	Tsp	Cumin
		Salt (to taste)

TUBLAH

1/4	Medium	Onion
1	Medium	Red bell pepper

Grind together. You can grind fresh or use previously frozen mixture.

Directions

You can use left-over kibbe Nayeh, or make from scratch. (see recipe for Kibbe Nayeh). If making from scratch it is not necessary to use organic meat unless you choose to do so.

If using leftover kibbe Nayeh, add more bulgur to the mix. This will hold the meat together once it is baked.

If making kibbe Syniah from scratch, follow the recipe for Kibbe Nayeh but add additional bulgur. If putting pine nuts in the center, saute the nuts in butter or ghee for just a couple of minutes. Any longer and they will burn.

You can also stuff the center with lamb and pine nuts. To do this saute the pine nuts and set aside. Brown lamb meat in butter until brown. Salt taste. Mix with pine nuts and layer on half the meat as instructed above.

Place half the meat mixture into a baking pan greased with olive oil. Place a layer of pine nuts on top, then place a top layer of meat mixture. Cut into small squares. Pour some olive oil on top to keep moisture in and to give it a nice brown look.

Bake at 425 degrees for 40 minutes or until done.

Kibbe bi Laban

Kibbe Balls in Yogurt

Ingredients

Servings:		7
Prep time:		30 minutes
Cook time:		40 minutes

KIBBE NAYYA RECIPE

20	Medium	Kibbe balls

YOGURT SAUCE

1	Qt	Yogurt
1	Medium	Egg white
1/4	Cup	Rice
1	Tbls	Cornstarch
2	Medium	Garlic cloves (minced)
2	Tbls	Olive oil (EVOO)
1/2	Cup	Water (boiling)

Directions

Put yogurt into a large pot.

Add the egg and cornstarch and whisk until well blended.

Place on medium heat and keep stirring clockwise until it starts to bubble.

If the yogurt base is too thick add the boiling water and stir, then gradually adjust the heat to low and let it simmer for 5 minutes

Add raw kibbe balls and let cook, about 30 minutes

While kibbe is cooking, add oil and garlic and stir for one minute on medium heat

Blend garlic and oil mixture with the yogurt base and stir until blended well.

Simmer for 3 minutes and turn off the heat.

NOTE: If using cooked kibbe balls, add to yogurt sauce and let heat for one minute before serving.

Arras Kibbe
Stuffed Kibbe Balls

Ingredients

Servings: 30
Prep time: 1 1/2 hours
Cook time: 30 minutes

KIBBE

1	Lb	Lamb or beef (I prefer beef)
1 1/2	Cups	Bulgur wheat (#1 or fine)
		Tublah (see recipe for Kibbe Nayeh)
3	Tsp	Allspice
1	Tsp	Cumin
		Salt (to taste)

FILLING

1	Lb	Lamb
1	Tsp	Allspice
1/2	Tsp	Cinnamon
		Salt to taste
1/2	Cup	Pine nuts
		Oil, ghee or butter for frying

Directions

In a bowl, soak the bulgur for 30 minutes.

In a large skillet add butter, ghee or oil and brown lamb meat. Remove from heat and add spices and pine nuts.

Mix kibbe as you would normally adding all listed ingredients.

Prepare a bowl of ice water to keep at your work station.

Take approximately 3 tablespoons of kibbe mixture and roll the size of a golf ball.

Place ball in one hand and with finger of the other hand poke a small hole in one end of ball. Gently roll the ball back and forth in your hand while pressing finger in circular motion. Keep doing this until the hole is large enough to place filling.

Scoop about 3/4 of a teaspoon of the filling and fill the hole. Do not overstuff. Dip fingers in ice water to aid in closing the end. Close the end by rolling the ball until the opening is small enough to close. Place finished balls onto parchment paper and refrigerate until firm.

You can bake or fry. If you fry, put enough oil in the pan to cover the ball. Place on medium high heat and add balls when oil is hot. Cook for one to two minutes until they turn a golden brown, then lower heat to medium and cook another three to four minutes until meat is cooked.

You can also bake in oven on greased sheet for 30-40 minutes at 350 degrees.

NOTE: You can use left-over Kibbe Nayeh, or make from scratch. (see recipe for Kibbe Nayeh). If making from scratch it is not necessary to use organic meat unless you choose to do so.

If using leftover Kibbe Nayeh, add more bulgur to the mix. This will hold the meat together once it is baked.

Kafta

Meat with Spices

Ingredients

Servings:		16 pieces
Prep Time:		20 minutes
Cook Time:		30 minutes
1	Lb	Ground Beef or Lamb
1	Medium	Onion (minced)
1	Tsp	Garlic (minced)
1/2	Cup	Parsley
1	Large	Egg
1/2	Cup	Bread Crumbs
1	Tsp	Salt
1	Tsp	Ground Allspice
1	Tsp	Paprika
1/4	Tsp	Aleppo Pepper
1/4	Tsp	Cumin

Directions

In a large bowl blend all ingredients and mix well.

Let sit for about 30 minutes to allow spices to be absorbed.

Form into small oblong shaped around a wooden skewer.

Bake or grill until done.

If baking set oven at 375 degrees for about 30 minutes.

If grilling cook about 15 minutes (depending on the size of the ball)

NOTE: You can substitute cilantro for parsley.

NOTE: I've found grilling to be better but baking is definitely an option

Lahem Meshwi
Skewered Lamb with Vegetables

Ingredients

Servings:		8-10
Prep Time:		2 hours
Cook Time:		10 minutes
3	Lbs	Lamb
3	Medium	Onion, quartered
5	Medium	Tomatoes
3	Large	Peppers, Green or red
1	Cup	Red wine
2	Tbls	Olive oil
		Salt and pepper to taste

Directions

Cut lamb into 1 inch cubes.

In a large bowl blend wine and oil and marinade meat for 2 hours.

Season with salt and pepper and place on skewers alternating meat, onions, peppers and tomatoes.

Cook on grill or under broiler in oven for approximately 10 minutes.

Serve with rice or salad and Lebanese bread.

NOTE: This may also be made with chicken (shish tawook) or beef (shish kabob)

Il Seine
Boiled Lamb's Tongue

Ingredients

Servings:		6
Prep Time:		20 minutes
Cook Time:		3 hours

3	Lbs	Fresh lamb's tongue
3	Cloves	Garlic
1		Bayleaf
		Salt and pepper to taste

Directions

Wash lamb tongue.

Please in pot and cover with water.

Bring to boil.

Discard water and cover with fresh water. Add garlic, bayleaf, salt and pepper.

Cook for 3 hours.

Skin, slice and serve with tahini sauce, salad, and spicy potatoes.

Baba Ghannouj
Eggplant with Tahini

Ingredients

Servings:		4
Prep Time:		15 minutes
Cook Time:		30 minutes (for eggplant)

Tahini Sauce Recipe, Page 50

1	Large	Eggplant (roasted)
½	Cup	Lemon juice
1	Clove	Garlic (peeled and whole)
½	Cup	Tahini
1	Tsp	Salt or more to taste
3	Tbls	Olive oil (add more as you blend if needed)

Directions

Roast unpeeled eggplant over open flame on gas range, under a broiler, or outdoor grill, turning often with tongs until skin is charred and blackened on all sides. Eggplant should be softened wherever you poke it. (about 30 mins)

Place eggplant on a paper towel, peel off skin removing all charred pieces. Place in a colander to drain thoroughly. Press down a little to make sure it is drained.

In a blender, place eggplant, lemon juice, whole garlic clove, olive oil, tahini and salt. Use a spatula to push down mixture and blend until smooth.

Put in a bowl, cover and chill.

When ready to serve, place in a bowl, drizzle with a little olive oil, and sprinkle a little paprika.

Serve with Lebanese bread or veggies.

Hummus
Chickpea and Tahini Dip

Ingredients

Servings:		6
Prep time:		20 minutes
Cook time:		No cooking

2	Cans	Chickpeas (drained and rinsed). Set aside liquid
1	Tbls	Olive oil
4	Tbls	Tahini
2	Tbls	Lemon juice (to taste)
1	Tsp	Garlic (chopped and to taste)
1	Tbls	Liquid from Chickpeas (add more to obtain a smooth consistency)

Directions

Put all ingredients in high speed blender or food processor and blend until smooth consistency. Add water if needed as you blend.

Serve with toasted pita chips or vegetables.

Toum
Garlic Sauce Dip

Ingredients

Servings: 8
Prep time: 20 minutes
Cook time: No cooking

48	Cloves	Garlic
2	Tsp	Salt
3	Cups	Oil (Canola, or highly refined Olive oil)
1/2	Cup	Lemon juice

Directions

Put garlic (no green parts) and salt in food processor.

Blend until garlic is completely pulverized.

Slowly pour in oil, one tablespoon at a time, while blending in food processor. This is a crucial step in creating the proper consistency.

Add lemon juice and blend.

It should have consistency of spreadable butter.

Served most often as a dip with pita chips.

NOTE: Very important. If you are using an olive oil, you want one that does not have a strong taste so as not to compete with the garlic.

Laban wa Khyar
Prepared Yogurt Sauce

Ingredients

Servings: 6
Prep time: 10 minutes
Cook time: No cooking

1	Cup	Laban
1	Cup	English cucumber (finely chopped)
1	Medium	Lemon
2	Cloves	Garlic, minced
1/2	Tsp	Fresh mint
1	Tsp	Fresh parsley
1/4	Tsp	Salt and pepper to taste
1/4	Cup	Ice cold water, add more as needed

Directions

In a bowl put laban, cucumber, garlic, water and mix. Do not beat.

Add fresh mint, lemon, salt and pepper.

Adjust herbs and spices according to your taste.

Sprinkle with parsley and drizzle with olive oil.

Serve with vegetables or pita chips or as a dipping sauce for skewered meats.

Tahini Sauce

Tahini Sauce

Ingredients

Servings: 5
Prep Time: 10 minutes
Cook Time: 10 minutes

1 1/2	Cups	Tahini (toasted sesame paste)
2	Cloves	Garlic
3/4	Cups	Lemon juice
1/2	Cup	Water (cold)
1/2	Tsp	Salt

Directions

Whisk tahini, garlic, lemon juice and salt until blended. Slowly add water. Keep whisking until lumps are gone and it has a creamy consistency.

Bite N,jan Mitla

Fried Eggplant

Ingredients

Servings:		4
Prep Time:		40 minutes
Cook Time:		20 Minutes
2	Lbs	Medium half peeled eggplant (or six eggplants)
1	Tsp	Salt
		Olive oil (for frying)

Directions

Slice eggplant and place on paper towel.

Sprinkle evenly with salt.

Let stand for 30 minutes. This will "sweat" the eggplant and drain moisture.

In a deep-frying pan heat oil and fry eggplant until it is light brown in color.

Place on paper towel for 10 minutes to absorb excess oil.

Serve with salad or meat dish.

Batoto harra
Lebanese Spicy Potatoes

Ingredients

Servings:	6
Prep Time:	15 minutes
Cook Time:	40 minutes

2	Tbls	Olive Oil
1/2	Tsp	Sea salt
2	Lbs	Potatoes, peeled and cut into cubes

SAUCE

4	Tbls	Olive oil
3	Cloves	Garlic
1/2	Tsp	Sea salt
1	Tsp	Paprika
1	Medium	Lemon wedges
1	Tsp	Chili Flakes
1/2	Tsp	Cayenne pepper
1/8	Tsp	Black pepper
		Mint (optional)

Directions

Preheat oven to 400 degrees F.

Peel and chop potatoes into cubes. Place the potatoes in large mixing bowl. Add the olive oil and salt to toss and coat them.

Line baking trays with parchment paper or spray them with non-stick spray.

Spread the potatoes in an even layer on the baking sheets. Bake for 20 minutes, flip potatoes and bake for another 20 minutes, until golden brown and crispy.

Remove potatoes and set aside.

In a large skillet heat the olive oil over medium heat. Add the garlic for one minute. Add the salt, paprika, cayenne pepper, chili flakes, and black pepper. Saute for another minute stirring.

Add the potatoes to the skillet and mix with the sauce. Remove from heat. Add mint (optional).

Serve salad, bread, and warm with lemon wedges.

Marshooshe

Cracked Wheat with Cabbage

Ingredients

Servings: 4
Prep Time: 20 minutes
Cook Time: 50 minutes

1	Cup	Bulgur (Medium)
1	Head	Cabbage
1/3	Cup	Olive Oil
1	Large	Onion
1	Tsp	Salt
1/2	Tsp	Black pepper

Directions

Wash bulgur two to three times in warm water. Let it soak in last wash for 30 minutes.

Wash cabbage and shred either by hand or in food processor.

Heat olive oil in large pan and fry onion until golden brown, about 10 minutes.

Add cabbage, cover and let fry on medium to low heat for about 15 minutes.

Stir frequently to avoid burning. Uncover pan and let cook for another 10 minutes.

Add bulgur and stir.

Add salt, pepper, and cover again and cook for another 15 minutes. Stir only one time.

Serve warm as a side dish or with Lebanese bread as a main dish.

Falafel
Chickpea Patty

Ingredients

Servings:		12 patties
Prep Time:		30 minutes once chickpeas are ready
Cook Time:		35 minutes

2	Cups	Chickpeas (dry)
1 1/2	Cups	Fresh parsley (curley leaf)
1	Small	Onion
6	Large	Garlic cloves
2	Tsp	Sesame seeds
1	Tsp	Salt
1	Tsp	Pepper (white)
1	Tbls	Cumin
1	Tsp	Cayenne pepper

Directions

Soak chickpeas overnight.

In large pot, add chickpeas and cover with broth (lamb or beef). Cook for four hours on stovetop.

Once chickpeas are thoroughly cooked add salt and let cool.

In mixer, add chickpeas, parsley, onion, garlic cloves, salt, pepper, cumin, cayenne, and sesame seeds. Blend until all ingredients are mixed.

If mixture is too moist, add 1/2 Tbls flour.

Form into patties (about the size of a hamburger patty).

Put patties in olive oil and bake on parchment sheet at 350 degrees for 35 minutes or fry in olive oil until golden brown.

NOTE: My grandmother preferred a patty rather than a ball as it works better if you plan to stuff into Lebanese bread.

Lifit makboos
Pickled Turnips

Ingredients

Servings: 10
Prep Time: 1 week; 3 days
Cook Time: None

5	Lbs	Turnips
1	Cup	Salt
1	Clove	Garlic
1	Large	Beet
1	Tbls	Vinegar
1	Gallon	Jar

Directions

Wash turnips and trim off stems and peel.
If turnips are too large cut in quarters otherwise cut in half.
Put turnips in salt and leave for 3 days. After third day drain liquid.
Put 1 teaspoon of salt and garlic clove in large jar.
Cook beet and cool, cut in half, then place in jar.
Fill jar with cold water.
Add vinegar and cover jar loosely.
Let stand for one week.

Macaroon bi toum
Lebanese Dumplings

Ingredients

Servings: 2-4
Prep Time: 30 minutes
Cooking Time: 15 minutes

Dumplings.
2	Cups	Flour
3/4	Cups	Lukewarm water
1	Tsp	Salt

Garlic Sauce:
6	Large	Garlic Cloves
1/2	Cup	Lemon juice (freshly squeezed)
1/3	Cup	Olive Oil (Start with this and add more as needed)
1/2	Tsp	Salt (Adjust to your taste)

Directions

TO MAKE DUMPLING DOUGH:

In a bowl mix flour and salt.

Slowly pour in water to make a dough. Wrap and set aside for 30 minutes.

On a lightly floured surface, roll into long ¼ inch thick rolls.

Cut into 1 inch pieces to form dumplings

Place on a floured cookie sheet and freeze without allowing pieces to touch. When frozen, place in a container and keep airtight in the freezer until ready to use.

Boil a large pot of water. When it comes to a boil, add 1 Tbls. of olive oil to water and ½ tsp. Salt.

Drop in dumplings (frozen) and bring to a boil again and cook until tender. The dough should float to the top. Check for tenderness.

When done, drain well.

Pour room temp garlic sauce over the dumplings and mix well. Add more olive oil and salt if necessary.

Optional: sprinkle with a little dry mint or finely chopped parsley (for presentation not flavoring)

TO MAKE GARLIC SAUCE

In a blender, mix together garlic with salt. Blend in lemon juice until well combined.

Slowly add the olive oil while blending until smooth and creamy.

Our Ancestors

Malcoun - Jacobs

Great- Grandparents

Jemila Maatouk Abdallah
Born 1862; Died 1948
wife of
Youssef Yaoub Abdallah
Mother to
Kature Michael (Jacobs)

Youssef Yaoub Abdallah
Born unknown, Died 1927
husband of
Jemila Maatouk Abdallah
Father to
Kature Michael (Jacobs)

Great- Grandmother

Najia Khoury, wife of Charbel Malcoun
Mother to Wadee Michael (Malcoun)
Born 1867; Died 1934

Grandparents

50th Wedding Anniversary, 1963
Wadee Michael (Malcoun) and Kature Michael (Jacobs)
Wadee - Born 1896; Died 1973
Kature - Born 1896; Died 1991
Children
Joseph, James, Emily, Mamie, Hazel

Malcoun/Jacobs

Joseph Michael
B: 1918; D: 2019

Emily Rishwain
B: 1920; D: 2014

James Michael
B: 1922; D: 2022

Mamie Pollock
B: 1925; D: 2010

Hazel Michael
B: 1927--

50th Wedding Anniversary, 1963
Wadee Michael (Malcoun) and Kature Michael
(Jacobs) From left to right:
Mamie, Hazel, Emily, James, Joseph

Descendants of Wadee and Kature Michael

Reunion, 2007
Family of
Wadee Michael (Malcoun) and Kature Michael (Jacobs)
Wadee and Kature had twenty-two grandchildren
(not all pictured)

Our Ancestors

Sassine - Courey

Great- Grandmother

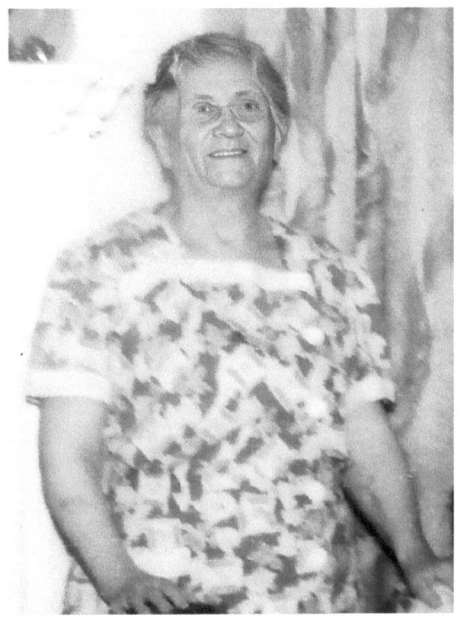

Warda Al Arn, wife of Sarkees Courey (Khoury)
Mother to Manilia Michael (Courey)
Born 1873; Died 1961

Grandparents

50th Wedding Anniversary, 1958
Joseph Michael (Sassine) and Manilia Michael (Courey)
Joseph - Born 1890; Died 1962
Manilia - Born 1893; Died 1979

Children
Nahia, Thomas, Michael, Margaret, John, Joseph, Janet

Sassine/Courey

Nahia Matte
B: 1909; D: 2003

Thomas Michael
B: 1912; D: 1983

Margaret Rishwain
B: 1918; D: 2002

Michael Michael M.D.
B: 1920; D: 2013

John Michael
B: 1923; D: 1962

Joseph Michael
B: 1925 D: 2012

Janet Kardoos
B: 1928; D: 1982

50th Wedding Anniversary, 1958
Joseph Michael (Sassine) and Manilia Michael (Courey)
From left to right:
Thomas, Michael, Margaret, John, Janet, Nahia, Joseph

50th Wedding Anniversary, 1958
Joseph Michael (Sassine) and Manilia Michael (Courey)
Joseph and Manilia had 26 grandchildren
(Not all are in the picture. Some were not born yet.)

Samke Hurro
White Fish with Tahini

Ingredients

Servings:		5
Prep Time:		30 minutes
Cook Time:		4 1/2 hours

Tahini Sauce Recipe, Page 50

5	Fillets	White fish
2	Tbls	Olive oil
1	Tsp	Salt or to taste
1	Tsp	Ground black pepper
1	Tsp	Cayenne
2	Tbls	Pine nuts
1	Tbls	Parsley for garnish
		Lemon Slices

Directions

Preheat the oven at 350 degrees F.

Place fish fillets in a baking dish - ensure the fish isn't crammed in the tray.

Sprinkle the fillets with olive oil, salt, pepper, and cayenne and place lemon slices on top and bake for 10 minutes, or until fish is just half cooked. Remove the baking dish from oven, cover and keep warm.

In a mixing bowl, combine 2 crushed garlic cloves, lemon juice, water, (you can add more lemon juice) pinch of salt, stir, and adjust by mixing in more water until it reaches the desired creamy mixture.

Prepare tahini sauce and pour it over the fillets and bake for about 15 to 20 minutes.

Remove from oven. Sprinkle pine nuts and parsley on top then serve it with baked potato alongside.

Yushar al'asmak
Fried Smelts

Ingredients

Servings:	4
Prep Time:	10 minutes
Cook Time:	6-8 minutes

2	Lbs	Smelts (about 36 smelt)
½	Cup	Flour for coating fish
1	Tsp	Salt
1	Tsp	Black pepper
½	Tsp	Paprika
1/2	Cup	Olive oil (for frying)

Directions

Thoroughly clean smelts (if not already clean by removing head and entrails. No need to remove bones before cooking unless it is your preference.

Wash and dry smelts.

Mix flour, salt, black pepper, and paprika together in a bowl or a bag.

Dust smelts with flour mixture completely on both sides.

Heat olive oil until it is very hot.

Drop smelts into pan and fry on medium high heat. Cook in small batches so they are not crowded in the pan.

Each side should take approximately 3-4 minutes to cook to a golden brown.

Once cooked place on paper towel to absorb excess oil. Sprinkle with additional salt before serving if you desire.

Serve with salad, homemade French fries, and Lebanese bread.

Tabouli

Parsley and Cracked Wheat Salad

Ingredients

Servings: 8
Prep Time: 30 minutes
Cook Time: None

5	Bunch	Parsley
3	Bunch	Green Onions
1	Bunch	Mint
4	Large	Tomatoes
1	Cup	Bulgur wheat (#1 or fine is best)
4	Medium	Lemons
1/4	Cup	Olive Oil
		Salt to taste

Directions

Wash wheat and let soak a bit to soften.

Chop parsley, onions, mint, and tomatoes by hand or in chopper (should be very fine). Add bulgur.

Squeeze fresh lemons. If lemons are on the large-side you may only need 3. Use according to taste.

Add olive oil, salt, and mix all.

Serve with Lebanese bread, lettuce, or grape leaves as scoops.

Fattoush
Lebanese Salad with Fried Pita Bread

Ingredients

Servings: 8
Prep Time: 30 minutes
Cook Time: None

Salad:

3	Loaves	Lebanese Bread or pita chips
2	Heads	Romaine lettuce
1	Large	Cucumber
3	Medium	Tomatoes
1/2	Bunch	Parsley
1/2	Bunch	Green onions
1/2	Bunch	Mint

Dressing:

1	Tsp	Salt
1/2	Tsp	Pepper
1	Tsp	Garlic (chopped)
3	Large	Lemons (juiced)
1/2	Cup	Olive oil

Directions

Toast Lebanese bread or pita chips until golden brown. Break into bite sized pieces.

Chop cucumber, lettuce, tomato, parsley, green onion, and mint into small pieces.

Thoroughly mix.

Add toasted bread and mix.

Mix all ingredients for dressing.

Add dressing to salad just before serving.

Bunuduro-Basal Sloto

Tomato and Onion Salad

Ingredients

Servings: 8
Prep Time: 20 minutes
Cook Time: None

6	Large	Tomatoes
2	Medium	Onions
2	Tbls	Dried mint (I use fresh, in season)
1	Tsp	Garlic powder
1/4	Cup	Olive Oil
		Salt and pepper to taste

Directions

Chop onions and tomatoes.
Mix with mint, garlic powder, salt and pepper.
Mix, using enough olive oil to coat the salad.
Serve while cold.

May be served with any main dish as a side.

Sloto Hindbee
Dandelion Salad

Ingredients

Servings: 4
Prep Time: 20 minutes
Cook Time: None

1	Lb	Dandelion leaves
1	Medium	Lemon, juiced
1	Clove	Garlic
1/8	Cup	Olive Oil
		Salt and pepper to taste

Directions

Wash leaves and squeeze moisture out thoroughly.

Chop leaves coarsely.

Add salt and mix. If moisture is still present, squeeze again.

Add oil, lemon juice, garlic, and onions and mix.

Laban
Yogurt

Ingredients

Servings: 6
Prep Time: 15 minutes
Cook Time: 40 minutes

2	Quarts	Milk
3	Tbls	Commercial yogurt (starter)
1	Heavy	Towel

Directions

Place milk on low fire and bring to slow boil.

Once it boils, remove immediately from heat and allow to cool to lukewarm. You should be able to immerse your finger and count to ten without it burning you.

Place starter into warm milk and thoroughly mix.

Wrap pan with heavy towel and set in warm space for 6-8 hours.

The freshly made yogurt should be jelled. Allow to sit for an hour then refrigerate.

NOTE: It's best to use fresh commercial yogurt (starter) if you want your Laban to be on the sweeter side.

Labneh
Pressed Yogurt

Ingredients

Servings: 2 cups
Prep Time: 10 minutes
Cook Time: Drain overnight

1	Quart	Homemade or commercial laban
1/4	Tsp	Fine grain sea salt

Directions

Take freshly made yogurt or commercial yogurt, add salt and place in a muslin bag or wrap securely in a cheesecloth.
Hang bag over bowl. Do not let it sit in the bowl.
Cover bag and bowl and place in the refrigerator for 24 hours. You can drain longer if you want a thicker consistency.

Remove from muslin bag and place in container in refrigeration. This should last about two weeks.

Jibneh

Lebanese Soft Cheese

Ingredients

Servings: 6
Prep Time: 40 minutes
Cook Time: No cooking

1	Gallon	Whole milk (not ultra pasteurized)
1/2	Cup	White vinegar
3	Tsp	Salt

Directions

Pour milk into a large pot and heat over high until reaching a boiling point, making sure to stir the milk to keep it from scorching.

Reduce heat to low and slowly add the white vinegar. You will immediately notice the curds separating, if for any reason the separation is not visible, add 1 tablespoon white vinegar. Set aside.

Line a colander with a cheesecloth over a large bowl, to catch the whey, don't discard the whey (the yellowy liquid dripped in the bowl) we will need them later to brine your cheese in. Using a spider spoon, ladle out the curds; pile them in the cheesecloth. You may need to do that repeatedly until there are no more visible solids. You grab the ends of the cheesecloth and wrap into a ball form to fully embrace the curds, twist to squeeze as much fluids as you can, the more you squeeze the better, but beware if it is too hot to handle. Put a heavy object, like a book, on top of the cheese to get rid of the excess liquid. Place the cheese in a bowl, the cheese will set and take the shape of whatever bowl or plate you place it in. Keep it for 15 minutes no more. Unwrap the cheese. Strain the whey: set a fine sieve lined with strong kitchen paper towels or a coffee filter over a large bowl, strain it to make it more clear. Transfer 3 cups of the whey to a saucepan and bring to boil. Add the salt, stir well to homogenize the mix. Set aside to completely cool down. Transfer the cheese block to a deep container and pour the whey, covering the cheese. Alternatively, you can cut the cheese to medium sized squares before covering with the whey. Refrigerate and eat eat within 2 weeks.

Rakakat Jibneh
Filo Stuffed with Cheese

Ingredients

Servings: 50 servings
PrepTime: 40 minutes
Cook Time: 20 minutes

1	Lb	Filo dough
1	Lb	Ricotta cheese
1	Lb	Mozaerella cheese (grated)
3	Large	Eggs
2	Stalks	Green onions (chopped fine)
1/4	Bunch	Parsley
1	Lb	Clarified butter
		Salt and Pepper to taste

Directions

Mix cheeses, eggs, onions, parsley, salt and pepper.

Cut filo dough into quarters.

Using two sheets, butter, then add 1 tsp of filling in one end and roll folding in sides. Bake at 350 degrees for 20 minutes or until edges start to turn golden brown.

NOTE: These can be frozen for later use. If freezing place in plastic freezer bag in rows with parchment paper in between layers. When cooking do not thaw before baking.

Laham Bidat
Lamb and Eggs

Ingredients

Servings:	4
Prep Time:	15 minutes
Cook Time:	10 minutes

8	Large	Eggs
1/2	Lb	Minced Lamb (add more or less based on preference)
1	Tsp	Salt
1/2	Tsp	Pepper
3	Tbls	Olive oil

Directions

Mince lamb but not too fine. I generally buy boneless lamb, mince it and freeze in portions for cooking.

Cook minced lamb in olive oil until nearly done. Set aside.

Whisk eggs in a bowl and add to same pan as used to cook lamb.

Scramble until half done, then add lamb.

Add salt and pepper. You can add more based on your preference.

Cook until done.

Serve while hot.

NOTE: Lamb and eggs were served in our home with fresh Lebanese bread and fresh sliced vegetables.

Ghejjeh

Lebanese Omelette

Ingredients

Servings: 12 fritters
Prep Time: 20 minutes
Cook Time: 15 minutes

1/2	Bunch	Parsley (chopped)
1/4	Cup	Mint leaves (chopped)
4	Minced	Green onions
1	Medium	Zucchini (grated)
6	Large	Eggs
1/4	Cup	Flour
1/2	Tsp	Allspice
1	Tsp	Salt
1/2	Tsp	Black pepper
1/4	Cup	Olive oil or avocado oil

Directions

After you wash and dry your vegetables, chop parsley, mint, green onions.

Grate zucchini. Set all vegetables aside.

In a large bowl, whisk eggs, flour and salt.

Add all vegetables including zucchini.

Chill mixture for 15 minutes. This allows the mixture to set for easier frying.

In a medium skillet, pour 1/4 cup oil. You can use olive or avocado for this.

Make sure oil reaches 350 degrees for best frying. Use a thermometer or drop a small scoop of mixture into pan. If it sizzles, the oil is hot enough.

Once oil is ready use a tablespoon or measuring cup to drop 1/4 cup of mixture into hot pan. Cook 3 to 4 minutes on first side. The edges should start to crisp.

Turn the patty when ready and cook for another 3 to 4 minutes.

Repeat until all vegetable mixture is cooked.

Set all fritters on a plate covered with a paper towel to absorb excess oil.

Serve with pita bread, sliced vegetables, and laban.

NOTE: If making Kousa, you can use the insides of the zucchini as a substitute for the zucchini. Use enough to equal two medium zucchinis. Or, you can substitute one potato.

Shrob
Rose Water Drink

Ingredients

Servings: 4
Prep Time: 20 minutes
Cook Time: 5 minutes

1	Cup	Water
3/4	Cup	Granulated sugar
1/4	Cup	Rose water syrup
3	Tbls	Rose water
1/4	Cup	Grenadine syrup

Directions

Pour sugar and water into saucepan.

Stir to combine over medium heat. Bring to a boil.

Simmer on reduced heat stirring occasionally until sugar is completely dissolved and clear. (about 5 minutes)

Turn off heat, cover and let syrup cool.

Add rose water syrup, rose water, and grenadine. (depending on your taste)

Serve over crushed ice. Garnish with mint.

*NOTE: This is a very sweet drink my grandmother used to make for us. You can dilute with water if you want less sweetness.

Laymun modo

Lebanese Lemonade

Ingredients

Servings: 7
Prep Time: 45 minutes
Cook Time: 1 1/2 hours

7	Medium	Lemons
1	Cup	Sugar
4	Cups	Water (May need more to dilute)
1	Tbls	Orange blossom water
2	Tbls	Rose Water
1/2	Bunch	Mint (for garnish)

Directions

In a large bowl, layer the lemon slices and sugar, alternating between the two until you've used up all the lemon slices and sugar. If you quartered the lemons, mix them well with the sugar until fully coated.

Use your hands, or a masher to mash the lemons to release some of their juices. Stir the juices with the sugar.

Cover the bowl and set the mixture aside for 30 minutes or ideally up to 24 hours in the fridge. Occasionally, pull it out and give everything a mash and a stir to dissolve the sugar.

After a while, the sugar will have dissolved and you will be left with a lemon syrup in the bottom of the bowl. Squeeze out the excess juice from the lemons and strain the lemon syrup through a fine mesh strainer. You should have about two cups of lemon syrup.

Place the lemons back in the bowl with two cups of water. Mash them again and stir together to release the remaining lemon syrup, then strain the mixture again.

Combine all the liquids together. You should now have a total of about 4 cups of lemonade concentrate. Store the concentrate in the fridge until you're ready to make lemonade.

Laymun modo
Continued

Directions

TO MAKE INDIVIDUAL GLASS OF LEMONADE:

Fill a glass with ice, half a cup of lemonade concentrate, and a quarter cup of water.

Stir, taste, and add more water as needed.

Then add half a teaspoon of orange blossom water and a splash of rose water if desired.

Taste and adjust to your preference.

TO MAKE A PITCHER OF LEMONDADE:

Fill a pitcher with ice, all of your lemonade concentrate, and two cups of water.

Stir, taste, and add more water as needed.

Then add one tablespoon of orange blossom water and two teaspoons of rose water if desired.

Taste and adjust to your preference.

NOTES
Storage: The lemonade concentrate can be stored in an airtight container in the fridge up to one week.

Zlabaya
Sugar Donuts

Ingredients

Servings: 8
Prep Time: 1 hour
Cook Time: 3-4 minutes per piece

4	Cups	Flour
1	Tsp	Salt
1	Tsp	Yeast (1 packet)
2	Tbls	Olive oil
1	Cup	Lukewarm water
1/2	Cup	Granulated sugar

Directions

Mix flour, salt, yeast, and oil with water.

Knead until mixed and let sit for one hour to rise.

Cut into strips of about 2" wide and 6" long.

Fry until golden brown and cooked through. Roll in granulated sugar.

Serve hot or cold.

NOTE: My grandmother used to twist them before frying. These were served traditionally at Easter time.

Ghriybah
Lebanese Sugar Cookies

Ingredients

Servings: 32 cookies
Prep Time: 20 minutes
Cook Time: 18-20 minutes

1	Cup	Ghee butter (room temperature)
1	Cup	Powdered sugar (sifted)
2	Cups	All-purpose flour
		Almond or pistachios (sliced)

Directions

Using a hand mixer put ghee and powdered sugar in a large bowl and mix for 5-7 minutes on medium-high speed. It should be light and fluffy.

Add in flour one-half cup at a time and mix with your hands.

Keep adding at 1/2 cup until all the flour is mixed well.

Form the dough into a round ball, cover and refrigerate for 45 minutes. (I've made them without refrigeration and they come out just fine.)

Form the dough into small balls. Press almond or pistachio into center (I use sliced almonds).

Bake at 350 degrees on the middle rack for 18-20 minutes. Bottoms should be slightly golden. Let them cool slightly before eating. I place them in a plastic bag, while warm, so they don't get hard.

Baklawa
Pastry with Sugared Nuts

Ingredients

Servings: 40 pieces
PrepTime: 30 minutes
Cook Time: 50-60 minutes

1	Lb box	Phyllo 9"x14" sheets room temperature
¾	Cup	Clarified butter or ghee
10	Cups	Walnuts or pistachios finely chopped
1	Cup	Powdered sugar

For the Simple Syrup

1	Cup	Granulated sugar
¾	Cup	Water
1	Tbls	Rose water
	Dash	Lemon

Directions

Combine nuts and sugar and mix thoroughly.

In a baking pan large enough to accommodate a full sheet of phyllo do, place one sheet of phyllo dough in the and butter the sheet. Continue to do this until you have half of the phyllo buttered.

Mix nuts with sugar and place mixture on dough and spread evenly, then dribble butter onto mixture.

Continue to layer and butter dough until the entire 1 lb dough is complete.
Cut tray into diamond shape.

Place in preheated oven at 350 degrees and bake for 50-60 minutes until golden brown.

To prepare syrup use boiling water to add to the sugar. Dissolve thoroughly and bring to a boil again.

Remove tray from oven. Add rose water and lemon to sugar syrup and pour immediately over entire tray.

Ma'moul

Date Stuffed Cookies

Ingredients

Servings: 48 cookies
Prep Time: 45 minutes
Cook Time: 30 minutes + 9 addl. minutes

2	Cups	Semolina flour
1	Cup	All purpose flour
1/2	Tsp	Mahlab
1/2	Tsp	Salt
1	Cup	Clarified butter (or ghee)
5	Tbls	Whole milk
2	Tbls	Sugar
1	Tsp	Dry yeast
4	Tbls	Orange blossom water
10	Tbls	Date paste
2	Tbls	Powered sugar (confectioner's sugar)

Directions

Preheat oven to 350 degrees. Line two baking sheets with parchment paper and set aside.
Mix semolina flour, all purpose flour, mahlab, and salt together.
Slowly mix clarified butter into the dry ingredients until thoroughly mixed.
Cover bowl and let rest overnight at room temperature.
Pour milk into a pan and heat until just barely warm. Remove from heat and place into a bowl.
Slowly stir in sugar and yeast until dissolved. Let sit until yeast foams, about 15 minutes.
Pour yeast mixture and orange blossom water over the dough and mix until moistened.
Pinch a piece of dough and roll into a ball. If it holds its shape without cracking the dough is properly prepared. You may add additional milk and/or orange blossom water if needed.
Cover and let rest for 15 minutes.
Using a ma'moul mold, sprinkle flour and tap out the excess.
Scoop a piece of dough and roll into a ball. Press your thumb into the dough and make a space for filling. Work the edges with your fingers so sides are even and thin. Drop a piece of date paste into opening and pinch closed to seal.
Place dough ball into the mold, seam side up. Press down so that the top is flush with edges of the mold. Trim excess dough, invert and tap against work surface to release cookie.
Repeat with remaining dough and arrange cookies 1 inch apart on prepared cookie sheets.
Bake one cookie sheet at a time until edges and bottoms are golden, about 15 minutes.
Sift powered sugar over cookies while still warm.

Family Favorites

The upcoming recipes may not be straight out of our village in Lebanon, but they do have a charming attachment to our village.

Cooked up on various occasions, from celebrations to just-because moments, these dishes hail from the same talented ancestral hands that lovingly prepared all the mouthwatering recipes you see in this book.

Each one proudly earns its spot in this culinary adventure.

Gram's Banana Cake

Ingredients

Servings: 8
Prep time: 15 minutes
Cook time: 40 minutes

CAKE

2 ¼	Cups	Flour
1 ½	Cups	Sugar
½	Cups	Crisco Shortening
1	Cup	Banana
1	Tsp	Baking soda
3	Tsp	Baking powder
½	Tsp	Salt
1	Cup	Milk
1	Tsp	Vanilla
2	Large	Eggs (slightly beaten)

FROSTING

Blend 1/2 cup powder sugar with 2 tablespoons of butter. Mix with enough cold milk to make a light, smooth icing. Add additional sugar if necessary to make the right consistency.

Directions

For cake, blend Crisco shortening with sugar.
In separate bowl, mix milk with flour.
Slowly fold in beaten eggs to the flour blend.
Blend all ingredients together.
Pour into greased cake pan.
Bake at 350 degrees for 40 minutes.
Once cooled, add icing and serve.

Gram's Lemon Meringue Pie

Ingredients

Servings: 6
Prep time: 30 minutes
Cook time: 10-12 minutes
9-inch deep dish pie plate

Crust:

1 ½	Cup	Sifted flour
1	Tsp	Salt
½	Cup	Shortening (Crisco)
4-5	Tbls	Ice cold water (optional carbonated soda: 7up, ginger ale, club soda; makes crust extra fluffy)

Lemon filling:

1	Cup	Sugar
2	Tbls	Flour
3	Tbls	Cornstarch
¼	Tsp	Salt
1 ½	Cups	Water
3	Medium	Lemons (juiced)
1	Tbls	Lemon zest (more if you like)
2	Tbls	Butter
4	Large	Egg yolks, beaten

Meringue:

4	Medium	Egg whites
6	Tbls	White sugar

Directions

FOR CRUST:

Sift together flour and salt. Cut in shortening ½ amount at a time until forms small pea sizes. Sprinkle 1T of water (soda) at a time and repeat until it is moist and forms a ball. Chill for about 15 mins. Covered.

Lemon Meringue Pie

continued

Roll out until about 1/8 inch thick.
Prick bottom and sides all around the pie shell.
Bake at 450 for about 10-12 mins or until golden brown.
Set aside to cool.

FOR LEMON FILLING:

In saucepan whisk together sugar, flour, salt, and cornstarch.
Stir continuously, add in water, lemon juice and zest.
Cook over medium heat until it comes to a boil, stir in butter.
In a small bowl of beaten egg yolks add slowly ½ cup of sugar mixture (slowly so yolks don't cook) whisk together, then add yolk mixture into the sugar mixture.
Bring to a boil and stir constantly until thick. Remove from heat and pour into prepared, baked pastry shell.

FOR MERINGUE:

In a large glass bowl, whip egg whites until foamy.
Gradually add sugar and continue to whip until it forms stiff peaks.
Spread over pie sealing to the edges at the crust, making peaks all over the meringue.
Bake in preheated 350 oven for 10 minutes until golden brown tips.

Aunt Margaret's Cheese Pie

Ingredients

Servings: 8
Prep time: 20 minutes
Cook time: 40-45 minutes

PIE CRUST

1 1/2	Cups	Graham cracker crumbs (ground fine)
2	Tbl	Butter (Melted)
1	Tbl	Sugar

FILLING

3	Logs	Cream Cheese
3/4	Cups	Heavy whipping cream
3	Large	Eggs
1	Cup	Sugar
1/2	Cup	Coffee Rich
2	Tbls	Vanilla

TOPPING

1	Pint	Sour Cream
1	Tbls	Sugar
1/2	Tsp	Vanilla
		Strawberries (optional)

Directions

For pie crust: Mix crumbs, butter, and sugar together. Form crust into 10" pie plate and freeze for 15 minutes.

For filling: Use food processor to mix cream cheese, eggs, sugar, and vanilla. Blend until very smooth and thick. Pour into pie shell. Bake at 350 degrees for 40-45 minutes. Allow to cool on rack for 6-8 minutes.

For topping: Mix by hand. Do not whip.

Spread mixture onto pie after it has cooled for 6-8 minutes. Be sure to push topping to the edges of the pie.

Return to oven and bake for 8-10 minutes.

Cool for 1/2 hour. Trim edges with extra graham cracker crumbs and place in refrigerator until completely cool.

Aunt Margaret's Chocolate Cream Pie

Ingredients

Servings: 8
Prep Time: 30 minutes
Cook Time: 12-15 minutes

1	Cup	Sugar
3	Tbls	Cornstarch
1/4	Tsp	Salt
2	Cups	Milk
1	Cup	Semi-sweet chocolate chips (add more is desired)
3	Large	Egg yolks (slightly beaten)
		Reserve egg whites
2	Tbls	Butter
1	Tsp	Vanilla extract

Directions

In a saucepan, combine first 3 ingredients, gradually add the milk mixing well.

Add chocolate chips. Cook and stir over medium heat until mixture thickens and boils. Cook about 2 mins longer stirring constantly.

Remove from heat. Stir in a small amount of hot liquid into 3 slightly beaten egg yolks. Immediately return to hot mixture stirring constantly over medium heat for 2 minutes.

Remove from heat add 2 T butter and 1 t vanilla and stir lightly.

Pour into 9 inch baked pie shell.

You can make a meringue with the egg whites and bake at 350 for 12-15 minutes and then cool pie.

NOTE: You can substitute cool whip for meringue.
You can use the same recipe, substituting a banana for chocolate to make banana cream pie

Aunt Nahia's Potato Cake

Ingredients

Servings: 8
Prep time: 50 minutes
Cook time: 30 minutes

1	Cup	Mashed potatoes (unseasoned)
1	Tsp	Cinnamon
1	Tbls	Nutmeg
3/4	Cup	Cocoa (Hershey's)
2/3	Cup	Crisco shortening
2	Cups	Sugar
4	Med	Eggs (unbeaten)
2	Cups	Flour
1	Cup	Chopped nuts
1/2	Cups	Milk
3	Tsp	Baking Powder
1/2	Tsp	Salt
1	Tsp	Vanilla

FROSTING:

2 1/2	Cups	Powdered sugar
1/4	Cup	Juice from one orange
		Grated orange skin
1/8	Tsp	Salt
1/2	Tsp	Vanilla
		Blend all ingredients until creamy

Directions

Boil potatoes and mash. Do not season. Gold potatoes work great.
Blend Crisco and sugar, and beat until fluffy little beads form.
Add eggs (one at a time) and mix together until creamy.
Add vanilla and potatoes.
Add dry ingredients together (salt, flour, baking powder, cinnamon, cocoa, and mix).
Add milk in separate bowl.
Alternate between adding milk and dry ingredients to the mixture. (about 1/4 of each at a time)
Beat until smooth, add nutmeg and 1/2 orange zest and mix thoroughly.
Place cake batter in greased and floured cake pan.
Bake at 350 degrees for 40 to 50 minutes.
Frost when cool. Garnish with other half of orange zest.

Aunt Hazel's Applesauce Cake

Ingredients

Servings: 8 servings
PrepTime: 30 minutes
Cook Time: 60 minutes

1	Cup	Sugar
2	Cups	Sifted Flour
1	Cup	Raisins (washed and drained)
4	Tbls	Hershey's Cocoa
1	Cup	Cracked Walnuts
1/2	Cup	Vegetable Oil
1	Tsp	Cinnamon
2	Cups	Applesauce
1/2	Tbls	Nutmeg
1/2	Tsp	Salt
1/2	Tsp	Baking Soda

FROSTING (optional)

8	Oz	Cream cheese
1/2	Cup	Butter
2	Tbls	Vanilla
4	Cups	Confectioner's Sugar

Blend all together and frost cake

Directions

Blend dry ingredients including sugar, flour, cocoa, cinnamon, nutmeg, salt and baking soda.

Fold in (slowly) oil, then add remaining ingredients including raisins, walnuts, applesauce. Bake at 300 degrees for one hour or until done. Press toothpick in center. If it comes out clean, it's done.

Beat cream cheese, softened butter, and vanilla together in a large bowl with an electric mixer until light and creamy.

Gradually fold in sugar and beat until smooth.

NOTE: Mom never frosted the cake when we were kids however, this frosting complements the cake very well.

Aunt Hazel's Pecan Pie

Ingredients

Servings: 6
Prep time: 30 minutes
Cook time: 45-50 minutes

1	9 in.	Pie crust (use store bought or recipe for lemon meringue crust)
1	Cup	Light corn syrup
1	Cup	Dark brown sugar (firmly packed)
3	Medium	Eggs (slightly beaten)
1/3	Cup	Butter (melted)
1/3	Tsp	Salt
1	Tsp	Vanilla
1	Cup	Pecans (heaping cup)

Directions

Prepare pie crust and place in pan.

Combine corn syrup, sugar, eggs, butter, salt, vanilla. Mix well.

Pour filling into pie crust.

Sprinkle pecans on top.

Bake at 350 degrees for 45 to 50 minutes, until center is set.

NOTE: Cover crust and top if pie gets too brown before it is completely baked. If you use and electric oven you may need to add an additional 15-20 minutes.

Contents - Lebanese Name

STUFFED STUFF
- Warak enyeb 16
- Mehseh Malfouf 17
- Koussa Mehseh 18
- M'Sorrin 19
- Ghammeh 20
- Sheikh el Mahshi 21

STEWS AND SOUPS
- Lubiah b'Lahem 22
- Fasolia bi Lahem 23
- Rishta 24
- Sharba djej ou riz 25
- Mudfunet Koussa 26
- Bite n'jan bi lahem 27
- Loubia b'zeit 28
- Djej Yakhnee 29

RICE DISHES
- Mujadara 30
- Hashawi 31
- Djej bi riz ou snoubor 32

BREADS
- Aajeen 33
- Khubez 34
- Mannoush 35

Contents - Lebanese Name

STUFFED BREAD PIES
Fatayer Spanigh... 36
Sfeeha.. 37
Lahem bi ajeen.. 38

MEATS
Kibbe Nayeh.. 39
Kibbe Syniah... 40
Kibbee bi Laban.. 41
   Kibbe Arras 42
Kafta.. 43
Lahem Meshwi.. 44
Il Seine.. 45

SAUCES AND DIPS
Baba Ghannouj... 46
Hummus.. 47
Toum.. 48
Laban wa Khyar.. 49
Tahini... 50

VEGETABLES AND DUMPLINGS
Bite N,jan Mitla 51
Batoto harra.. 52
Marshooshe.. 53
Falafel... 54
Lifit makboos.. 55
Macaroon bi toum... 56

Contents - Lebanese Name

FISH
    Samke Hurro.. 57
    Yushar al'asmak...................................... 58

SALADS
    Tabouli... 59
    Fattoush... 60
    Bunuduro-Basal sloto............................. 61
    Sloto Hindbee.. 62

YOGURTS AND CHEESES
    Laban... 63
    Labneh... 64
    Jibneh.. 65
    Rakakat Jibneh...................................... 66

EGGS
    Laham Bidat.. 67
    Ghejjeh.. 68

REFRESHMENTS
    Shrob... 69
    Laymun modo....................................... 70

Contents - Lebanese Name

DESSERTS

    Zlabaya.. 72

    Ghriybah.. 73

    Baklawa... 74

    Ma'moul... 75

FAMILY FAVORITES

    Grandma's banana cake.......................... 77

    Grandma's lemon meringue pie............... 78

    Aunt Margaret's cheese pie...................... 80

    Aunt Margaret's chocolate cream pie....... 81

    Aunt Nahia's potato cake......................... 82

    Aunt Hazel's applesauce cake................. 83

    Pecan pie.. 84

Photo Credits

Special Thanks to:

- Ben Rishwain
- Michelle Camping
- Caryn Rishwain Willet
- Mark Michael
- Brenda Matte Butler
- Denise Matte Zambeck
- Michelle Michael Scott
- Caryn Pollock

About the Author

Valerie Michael grew up with a deep respect for her Lebanese roots. Her inspiration for *A Taste Of Serhel* came from her desire to preserve her family's rich and long-standing history dating back generations to a small village in Lebanon. Her fondest memories as a little girl growing up in Grosse Pointe, MI are of the amazing foods prepared by her grandmothers and aunts and the large extended family that gathered often in celebration against a backdrop of these delicious and traditional Lebanese foods.

Valerie holds a Bachelor of Arts degree in Communications Studies from the University of Nevada, Las Vegas. She has over forty years of experience in Marketing and Communications, new business management, event planning, campaign management and crisis communications. Throughout her career she has won numerous awards for outstanding achievements and has developed programs still in use today worldwide. Valerie is retired but continues her lifelong commitment to community service and has volunteered for numerous industry, charitable, and political organizations.

Valerie currently resides in Northern Nevada.

www.ingramcontent.com/pod-product-compliance
Lightning Source LLC
Chambersburg PA
CBHW041134130526
44582CB00028B/113